Raymond Harris

A Scriptural Refutation of a Pamphlet

Lately Published by the Rev. Raymond Harris

Raymond Harris

A Scriptural Refutation of a Pamphlet
Lately Published by the Rev. Raymond Harris

ISBN/EAN: 9783744793575

Printed in Europe, USA, Canada, Australia, Japan

Cover: Foto ©ninafisch / pixelio.de

More available books at **www.hansebooks.com**

A

SCRIPTURAL REFUTATION

O F A

P A M P H L E T,

LATELY PUBLISHED BY THE REV. RAYMUND HARRIS,

I N T I T L E D,

" SCRIPTURAL RESEARCHES

O N T H E

LICITNESS. of the SLAVE TRADE."

In FOUR LETTERS from the AUTHOR
to a FRIEND.

———— " from love of grace
Lay not *his flattering unction* to your fouls."

L O N D O N.
Printed for B. LAW, Ave-Mary Lane, Ludgate Street.
MDCCLXXXVIII.

A

Scriptural Refutation, &c.

***

LETTER I.

I HAVE perufed with fome degree of attention, the very extraordinary pamphlet which you lately fent me, intitled, *" Scriptural Refearches on the* LICITNESS *of the Slave Trade, by the Rev. Raymund Harris ;"* in which the author has endeavoured to fhew *" its conformity with the principles of natural and revealed religion, as delineated in the facred writings of the word of God."*

B   Although

Although I have not that high opinion of the state of improvement, in this age and country, which many persons profess to entertain, yet I own I could not avoid being surprised, that either the one or the other, should have been insulted by the publication of a work, which, if its dangerous and destructive principles were admitted in their full extent, would shake the foundations of society, and establish, *by the sanction of divine authority,* every variety of oppression, and every species of guilt.

The short account you gave me of the character and profession of the author, operated however as a sort of comment on his work. The unnatural attachment to slavery—the aversion and dread of the interference of reason and common sense—the artful and subtle positions which are the foundation of his work, appear
totally

totally irreconcileable to the character of an *Englishman*, but are perfectly confiftent with that of *a Spanish Jefuit*.

I muft not, however, charge the Rev. Raymund Harris, with being the firft who has openly attempted the juftification of moral guilt, from the books of the old and new teftament. So long ago as the beginning of the 15th century, one *John Petit*, a doctor of the church in France, not only publicly juftified the murder of the Duke of Orleans, by the Duke of Burgundy, but took occafion, at the fame time, to affert the *general legality* (or, as it is now expreffed, the *licitnefs*) of homicide, which he founded on the example of all the murders mentioned in the old teftament, by making that *a rule of conduct*, which was only introduced as *a mere hiftorical narrative*.

As

As I have at prefent a little leifure, I think I cannot employ it to better pur-pofe, than in ftripping the mafk from this concealed enemy of order and religion, and expofing him to the world in his proper colours. But before I enter on the examination of his work, it may not be improper to premife, that I fhall con-fine myfelf to the mode of proof he has himfelf prefcribed; viz. *to that derived from the authority of the facred writings only* — not thinking it in any degree ne-ceffary in the refutation of his work, to refort to thofe more general arguments which are derived from the nature of man, and the univerfal principles of truth and juftice, as implanted in the human mind, by the immediate hand of its great author ; nor availing myfelf of an objec-tion, which might be reafonably made, viz. That in difcuffing a matter of right between the Europeans and the Africans,

an

an appeal is made to an authority, which one of the parties only acknowledges as legitimate.

But though I ſhall confine myſelf to the proofs and authorities deduced from the ſacred writings, yet I cannot ſo far coincide with Mr. H's wiſh, as entirely to diveſt myſelf of " *the ſcanty light of mere human reaſon and ſenſe*," which, notwithſtanding the opprobium thrown upon it by Mr. H. in his preface, I cannot help thinking, is in ſome degree neceſſary, to enable us to underſtand thoſe writings. Mr. H. indeed afterwards informs us, that he has prefixed to the whole of his work, a few poſitions or data, which he truſts will be found unqueſtionably true, and *exactly conformable to ſound reaſon*; and thus, whilſt in one breath he impeaches the authority of this ultimate

judge

judge of truth, in the next he admits it to queftion his firft principles.

With this permiffion then, I fhall, in the prefent letter, take the liberty of ftating a few of his data, (which are twelve in number) and trying whether they are confiftent with found reafon or not ; in which I fhall endeavour to be as concife as the nature of the fubject will admit.

His 1ft and 2d pofitions are,

> " *That the volume of the facred* " *writings, commonly called the Holy* " *Bible, comprehending both the Old* " *and New Teftaments, contains the* " *unerring decifions of the word of* " *God. That thefe decifions are* " *of equal authority in both the* " *Teftaments ; and that that au-* " *thority is the effential veracity of* " *God, who is truth itfelf.*"

Now

Now if we for a moment apply to thefe pofitions the touchftone of human reafon, we fhall find that fome of them are fundamentally falfe; and that all of them are to be underftood with many reftrictions and exceptions. That the Old and New Teftaments contain the unerring decifions of God, where God has exprefsly given them to us as his decifions, every Chriftian will readily admit; but it is obvious, that the far greater part of the Old and New Teftament, confifts, not of *decifions*, but *of mere hiftorical facts*, fome of them affording inftances of a virtuous, and others of a vicious conduct. That other parts of the fcriptures, even where fuch decifions are found, are not of general ufe, but are applicable only to *particular times, or to a particular people.* That *it is not true* that the decifions of the Old and New Teftament are of equal authority, for that the former is always controlled

by

by the latter; which has totally abrogated many parts of the Mosaic law, and made an essential difference, not only in the ritual, but in the moral duties injoined by the Old Testament, as I shall hereafter have occasion to shew more at large.

The essence of his four next positions is, *That whatever is declared to be right or wrong in the scriptures, is so in its nature, and cannot be questioned without great presumption; but must be assented to without reserve, however contrary it may be to the opinions of men for any length of time.* But these positions are also laid down in a form, much too general to be admitted by the professors of any religion, except that in which the reverend author was educated. It will readily be granted, that whenever the scriptures have decided on general principles of right and

wrong,

wrong, fuch decifions are unerring;
but it muft alfo be granted, that when
thofe decifions have a reference to the
fituation of a particular perfon, or a particular nation, they ought not to be arbi-
trarily and indifcriminately applied to other
perfons, or other nations : And if from
the powers given to the Jews over their
enemies, the permiffion of certain acts in
particular cafes, and the exiftence of certain cuftoms amongft them, we were to
infer a right in ourfelves, to imitate their
actions, and practife their cuftoms, whenever we thought there was a fimilarity in
our fituation, the book of the Old Teftament might be converted into a *general
voucher* for the *licitnefs* of almoft every
crime, and every enormity, whether na-
tional or individual.

Mr. H. proceeds in his 5th datum to
ftate, " *That if one or more decifions of*

C

" *the*

" *the written word of God give a*
" *positive sanction to the intrinsic*
" *licitness of any human pursuit, for*
" *instance, the Slave Trade, whoever*
" *professes to believe the incontro-*
" *vertible veracity of the written*
" *word of God essentially incompati-*
" *ble with the least degree of injustice,*
" *must consequently believe the pur-*
" *suit itself to be intrinsically just and*
" *lawful in the strictest sense of the*
" *word.*"

From this position then it would seem
that all actions which have, under the
Jewish dispensation, been practised by the
sanction of divine authority, are intrinsically and universally right, and may be
practised by all mankind, in all future
times, not only without guilt, but with
the strictest virtue and propriety; and this
most extensive rule is founded on a presumption,

fumption, that what God has, on one occafion, declared to be right, muft alfo be right on all other occafions, without any attention to the particular circum-ftances of each. Suppofing this pofition to be once granted, it is doubtful whether the depravity of man could commit a crime for which Mr. H. would not, from the facred writings, extract a better apo-logy than he has already done for the Slave Trade. Thus, for inftance, if any man doubted of the inherent licitnefs of

I N C E S T,

It would be eafy for Mr. Harris to point out the example of the daughters of Lot, who each of them conceived by their father,* which tranfaction, fo far from being reprefented as criminal, not only paffes free from the leaft fhadow of reprehenfion, but the offspring of this in-

C 2   tercourfe,

*Gen. c, xix. v. 30.

tercourfe, became the founders of two
powerful nations. Jacob's marrying
two fifters,* by each of whom he had
children, and who purchafed of each
other his favors,† would be an exprefs
authority. Were a doubt ftill entertained
of the licitnefs of the crime, Mr. H.
might refer to the general laws of the.
Jews, by which the furviving brother
was commanded to go in unto his
brother's wife, and marry her, and
raife up feed to his brother; and
might point out an inftance where a
refufal to comply with this injunction, brought down upon the offender
the immediate vengeance of God.‡ Mr.
H. might then advert to the ftate of mankind in the firft age of the world, when
the commiffion of this crime was not only
excufable, but indifpenfibly neceffary to
the prefervation of the fpecies, and thus
the

---

* Gen. c. xxix.   † Gen. c. xxx. v. 15.
‡ Gen. c. xxxviii, p. 8.

the inherent licitnefs of this heinous offence would be much more fatisfactorily proved than the lawful nature of the African Slave Trade, notwithftanding the indefatigable labour which Mr. H. has beftowed upon it.

F R A U D.

Should any perfon entertain fcruples of confcience, with refpect to the lawfulnefs of defrauding his neighbour, let him adopt Mr. H's pofition, and open the Old Teftament. He will there find that the patriarch Jacob, the immediate founder and ftock of the Jewifh nation, under pretence of a purchafe, defrauded his brother Efau of his birth right;* and in order to compleat this firft piece of treachery, was induced, by a contrivance of the moft artful nature, to obtain from his father Ifaac, the bleffing of the firft born,

* Gen. c. xxv, v. 29.

born, to the wrong and prejudice of his elder brother. Should he still remain doubtful, he may turn to another incident in the life of the same patriarch, related at large Gen. c. 30, v. 25. in which he will find a stratagem put in execution by Jacob to defraud Laban, his father-in-law, which, according to his position, will justify the inherent licitness of cheat-ing beyond the shadow of contradiction. To these authentic facts, which were the foundation of Jacob's greatness, he may add the authorities that may be deduced from Ex. c. xi, v. 2. and c. xii, v. 35. where the Is-raelites abused the confidence of the Egyp-tians, and deprived them of their jewels, by an express command of their great law-giver; and the evident conclusion of his *scriptural researches on the licitness of fraud* will be, that every man has an inherent right, by the express sanction of the holy scriptures, to defraud his neighbour; nay,

even

even his brother or his father, as often as
it lies in his power.

It would thus be practicable, under the
sanction of Mr. H's 7th position, to se-
lect, from the books of the Old Testament, the most evident and inconteftible
authorities, not only for the lawfulnefs of
lying, theft, polygamy, and fornication,
but of the more atrocious crimes of murder, adultery, and revenge; but it is irk-
fome to proceed further under the guid-
ance of *fo deteftable a propofition,* which,
under a pretence of paying an implicit
deference to the judgments of God, ex-
cludes every confideration of a collateral
nature, and thereby renders unjuft and
criminal in its general application, that
which in the particular inftance, and
under peculiar circumftances, was right
and lawful, and calls in the authority of
the

word of God to juftify the commiffion of crimes of the deepeft dye.

The remainder of the author's data are employed to ftate in various lights, *that if any act (e. g. the Slave Trade) be abftractedly and effentially lawful, no abufe or mal-practice can render the principle of it criminal; and that no arguments built folely on thofe abufes, can have any weight, unlefs the fame be proved effentially unjuft and illicit.*

To attempt a diftinction between the abftract nature of any thing and the effects produced by it, is well worthy one of the difciples of Loyola; but though thefe fubtleties might have paffed current in the days of our anceftors they are now fomewhat out of feafon. A fort of maxim has prevailed, that it is improper to reafon from the

abufe

abuſe of any given ſubject, againſt the uſe of it, but it will ſurely be granted, that a pronenefs to abuſe is itſelf ſtrong evidence that ſomething is wrong in the principle. It was not by ſubtle diſtinctions of this kind that our Saviour inſtructed his followers : He taught us to judge of the cauſe by its effects, and not to ſuppoſe that could be right in its principle which was manifeſtly wrong in its conſequences.—" *A good tree, ſays he, cannot bring forth evil fruit, neither can a corrupt tree bring forth good fruit; wherefore by their fruits ye ſhall know them,* Matt. chap. vii. v. 18, 20. What have been the fruits of the African Slave Trade I leave to the determination of Mr. H. who, by declining to ſubmit to this teſt, ſhews pretty clearly the ſenſe he entertains of the cauſe he has undertaken to defend.

D   From

From thefe remarks I truft it will evidently appear, that although the fcriptures contain the written will of God, yet, as in reading the facred volumes we muft ufe our eyes, fo, in underftanding them, we muft make ufe of our reafon. It is true, the Church of Rome prohibits its followers not only from confidering, but perufing the fcriptures; and requires them to be implicitly acknowledged as equally and invariably true in all parts: But the Proteftant Churches have difcarded thefe narrow reftraints, and not only permit, but require us to examine the fcriptures with the utmoft degree of attention and care. Shall we then fo far fuffer ourfelves to be blinded by the propofitions, or by the fubfequent denunciations of Mr. H. as to give up, at his fimple requeft, a right for which our anceftors ftruggled at the expence of their blood? Or fhall we not rather, like

like men and proteſtants, judge for our-
ſelves of the ſpirit and tendency of the
holy ſcriptures? Under this idea it will
then be neceſſary, before we ground our
conduct upon the precepts or examples
they afford us, diligently to examine whether ſuch examples and precepts are *of
general and univerſal import*, or only confined to a particular perſon or people.
Whether ſome things which are allowed
or commanded in the Old Teſtament
be not annulled or explained in the new,
and conſtantly to make the moſt accu-
rate diſtinction between ſuch paſſages as
ought to influence our conduct, and *ſuch
as are merely narrative.* By theſe means
we ſhall perceive, that it would be as
abſurd to aſſert that the inhabitants of
Great Britain can be juſtified in carrying
away the natives of Africa from their
country and friends to perpetual ſervitude, *becauſe* the Jews had domeſtic ſlaves

in

in their houſes, as to ſuppoſe that we have a right to deſtroy all the nations round us, *becauſe* Joſhua ſmote thirty-one kings on the other ſide of the River Jordan.*

---

* Joſh. c. xii. v. 7.

LETTER II.

I HAVE in my former letter fhewn, that the *data* required by Mr. H. are fuch as cannot be granted, without confiderable reftrictions upon their import, by any perfon who affumes the character of a proteftant, or profeffes to make ufe of his reafon in the examination of the fcriptures. In the prefent, I fhall point out in what manner his fubfequent arguments in favour of the Slave Trade, are affected by this correction of his firft principles.

Having ftated as a pofition, that every thing contained in the fcriptures is equally true,

true, and univerfally applicable; without any exception whatever of *perfon, time,* or *place,* or the confideration of *any concurring circumftance,* he proceeds to fhew, that the cuftom of flavery was permitted in the ancient world, and cites the particular examples of Abraham, Jofeph, and Jofhua, with many texts on the fubjects; occupying the greateft part of his pamphlet with demonftrating, what no one ever thought of denying, viz. *that the Jews were allowed to purchafe bond-men and bond-women of the heathen;* and under certain ftipulations to retain in their fervice, even thofe of their own country.

But it is furely fomewhat extraordinary, that fo acute a Logician, after having at fuch length laid down his premifes, and fanctioned them by fuch numerous appeals to holy writ, fhould be *fo miferably defective* in drawing his conclufions from them.

them. After having fhewn the *licitnefs* of Slavery to the Jews and their imme-diate anceftors, it might have been ex-pected, that the author would thence have deduced *the right of the Europeans to enflave the inhabitants of Africa;* but on this important head he is totally filent: and the whole of his reafonings, and re-fearches, are equally calculated to prove, *that the negroes have an inherent right to take us and our families and carry us into perpetual flavery,* as that we have *a right to purfue the African Slave Trade.*

That the Ifraelites had the permiffion of the Divine Being, to retain in their fervice bond-men and bond-women of the heathen, and even of their own na-tion, for a limited time, is granted; but this permiffion appears to have been par-ticularly confined to that nation, and was not extended to the reft of mankind:

Nor

Nor is there in Mr. H's researches, the least ground to conclude, that any particular nation succeeded to that extraordinary privilege over other nations, which was exercised by, and allowed to the children of Ifrael.*

Let us suppose then, that some particular person, accused of exercising a right which interfered with the welfare of his neighbour, should rise up before his judges, and inform them by many authorities, that the same right had been exercised by a certain person, at some former, but remote period of time; and having proved this, to the satisfaction of the court, should sit himself down, in complacent expectation of a decree in his favor.

---

* That the practice of *Man-stealing*, as the object of a general law, was considered, both under the old and new dispensation, as a crime of the higheft magnitude, may appear from Exodus c. xxi. v. 16. Paul's I. Epiftle to Tim. c. i. v. 9 and 10.

Would either the judges, or auditors, think him intitled to that decree, till he had alſo gone one ſtep further, and demonſtrated, that *he was the perſon who had legally ſucceeded to ſuch right?*

But perhaps Mr. H. will contend, that the permiſſion of retaining ſlaves *was not confined to the Jews*, but was a *general law*, extending to the whole human race. Now, though I ſhall by no means acquieſce in this conſtruction of the ſacred books, yet let us for a moment ſee what the author of the pamphlet would gain by ſuch a conceſſion.—The reſult would ſimply be, that by the *unerring deciſion of the great parent of the univerſe*, the ſtronger nation or individual would have an *inherent right* to oppreſs and reduce to ſervitude, the weaker. A ſuppoſition as injurious to the Divine Goodneſs, as any of thoſe, upon which Mr. H.

E

has

has beſtowed the epithets of blaſphemous
and preſumptuous.

Thus then you will perceive, that the
ordinances of God are ſometimes of a general nature, having reference to all mankind; and ſometimes of a particular nature, having reference only to the people to whom they are immediately delivered. That the firſt are uniformly and
invariably juſt and true, and that the ſe-
cond are alſo juſt and true, when applied
to the ſubject on which they are intended
to operate; but may become unjuſt, and
improper, when applied *at the will of man*
to other purpoſes, and on other occaſions.

As I apprehend this to be a diſtinction
of great importance in the preſent debate,
I ſhall take the trouble of giving you an
illuſtration of it; by ſhewing how differ-
ently

ently the principles required by Mr. H.
operate upon any given fubject, when admitted in their full extent, and when
taken with the reftrictions I have ventured
to lay upon them. Let this be taken from
the firft inftance mentioned in the pamphlet, and on which Mr. H. lays the great
weight of his caufe, afferting, " That were
" all other fcriptural evidences wanting in
" favor of the Slave Trade, this decree
" alone muft convince every impartial
" reader, that the *licitnefs* of that trade
" is evidently warranted by the written
" word of God."

The ftory is that of HAGAR* the hand-
maid of Sarai, who after fhe had conceived a fon by Abram her mafter, fled
from the fight of her miftrefs, becaufe
fhe dealt hardly with her; and was found
near a fountain of water in the wilder-
nefs, by an angel of the Lord; who or-

E 2   dered

* Gen. c. xvi.

dered her to return to her miſtreſs, and ſubmit herſelf under her hands, with a promiſe that the Lord would multiply her ſeed exceedingly.

Now in making the *particular inſtance* of God's dealings with Hagar (for which there is no doubt he had the beſt and wiſeſt reaſons) a *general rule*, to be applied on all ſimilar occaſions, Mr. H. attempts to eſtabliſh a mode of proof, which, if admitted, would tear up the foundations of ſociety;—introduce and ſanctify a courſe of conduct at open variance with the firſt laws of truth and juſtice, as derived from God; and render it eaſy to juſtify any crime which the moſt abandoned profligate might be induced to commit.

" Every circumſtance, ſays he, attend-
" ing the wretched ſituation of *this poor*
" *African*

" *African Slave,* who though *legally*
" *married to her mafter,* is kept ftill
" in bondage, and forced as it were out
" of his houfe and fervice, in the con-
" dition fhe was in *through hard ufage*
" *and feverity,* feems to excite compaf-
" fion, and juftify her efcape."

Having thus allowed the apparent injuftice of Hagar's fufferings, he proceeds.

" Were Hagar's cafe that of any Afri-
" can Female Slave now in the Weft-
" Indies, and were the fame to be tried
" before a jury compofed of *fome of the*
" *prefent advocates for African liberty in*
" *this ifland,* one might decide almoft to
" a certainty in whofe favor the verdict
" would be given : The flave would moft
" probably be declared free; and both
" mafter and miftrefs feverely repri-
" manded, if not alfo condemned in a
" heavy

" heavy pecuniary mulct. No other
" verdict would be confiftent with the
" principles *they fo publickly avow.*—But
" did HAGAR obtain the fame favorable
" fentence at the impartial tribunal of
" God, when fhe pleaded her caufe be-
" fore the minifter of his juftice, whom
" he deputed to reprefent his perfon ?
" Did 'he approve of her conduct in
" leaving her mafter's houfe, &c.? Did
" he fignify to her, that her character of
" Abram's wife, or the feverity of Sa-
" rah's treatment, even in her actual
" ftate of pregnancy, emancipated her
" from her bondage, refcinded the ori-
" ginal contract of her purchafe, or that
" that contract had been illicit, and
" contrary to his laws, &c.? No. On
" the contrary, her conduct was con-
" demned by the reprefentative of God,
" who ordered her in his name to return
" to her miftrefs, and fubmit herfelf un-

der

" der her hands; though at the fame
" time he affured her. *that the Lord had*
" *heard her affliction.*"

From this moft fingular comment Mr.
H. immediately concludes, " that the
" licitnefs of the flave trade is evi-
" dently warranted by the written word
" of God." But before we allow the
cafe of Hagar to be a fanction for a fubfequent courfe of conduct, of fo diffimi-
lar a nature, let us examine the deductions which Mr. H. in his foregoing comment has endeavoured to draw
from this ftory, and which he muft eftablifh before it can be of the leaft fervice
to the caufe it is introduced to fupport:
Thefe evidently are,

I. That in cafe the caufe of Hagar had
been tried before a juft and impartial
human tribunal, they would have been
culpable

culpable in deciding upon it according to the known laws of juftice and humanity.

II. That on all fubfequent occafions, where a perfon has fuffered under the rod of oppreffion, it is the bufinefs of a judge to fend back the fufferer to receive further ill treatment.

III. That becaufe Hagar was ordered by an angel to return to her miftrefs, it is lawful for the merchants of Europe to carry on a Trade for Slaves to the coaft of Africa.

I fhall clofe my prefent letter with a few obfervations on each of thefe deductions.

I. The Supreme Being alone can fearch the hearts of men, and the reafons of *his*
immediate

immediate determinations are not always apparent to his creatures, who can only form their imperfect judgment from external circumstances.—It was therefore no doubt confistent with his wifdom and juftice to direct Hagar's return. *He had power to foften the heart of her miftrefs towards her*, and to *recompenfe her obedience as he thought good*,—but would an earthly tribunal have been therefore excufable, in difcarding every principle of Juftice, and fending Hagar back to receive further ill treatment?—The idea is equally wicked and ridiculous.

II. It feems fcarcely poffible to conceive a higher degree of prefumption, than that of applying the *particular judgments* of God to fubfequent purpofes and occafions. That a cafe *exactly fimilar* in all points to that of Hagar, has ever fince happened, may very fairly be doubted; and until that does really happen,

F

pen,

pen, the decree of the Supreme Being *appropriated* to that cafe, can never again be applicable. Befides, the powers and faculties of our minds are not fufficiently extenfive, to enable us to judge of the circumftances in all their connections, even if fuch a cafe fhould again exift.— To reafon therefore from this inftance, to others which evidently bear only a *partial* or *diftant refemblance* to it, is the extreme of arrogance ; and to act in confequence of fuch reafoning, would be the extreme of wickednefs.

III. But from what circumftances in this ftory does Mr. H. deduce the very extraordinary conclufion, *That the Slave* " *Trade, even when attended with cir-* " *cumftances not altogether conformable* " *to the feelings of humanity,* is *effenti-* " *ally confiftent with the facred and in-* " *alienable rights of juftice, and has the* " *pofitive*

" *pofitive fanction* of God in its fup-
" *port*." What? Becaufe the Lord, by
his angel, ordered Hagar to return to
her mafter, to whom fhe was under fome
kind of obligation for fervice, whether
voluntary or involuntary does not appear,
to whom fhe was *legally married* and by
whom fhe was *then pregnant* ? Does it
by any rule of conftruction follow, that
Mr. H. or any other perfon, has *an inherent right*, either forcibly, or by the
colourable pretext of purchafe, to feize
upon an inhabitant of *Whidah*, or *Congo*,
whom *he had never before feen*, to carry
him on board a fhip, and expofe him for
feveral months to variety of dangers,
and if he furvives, to deliver him over
to a planter, to exhauft the remainder of his days in extreme labour, under *the immediate difcipline of the fcourge ?*
—Juftice, humanity, and common fenfe
equally revolt at fuch a deduction.—

But

But as Mr. H. has openly difclaimed all connection with thefe dangerous guides of human conduct, I fhall apply my remark in a different form; and affure him, that whenever a ftronger hand than his own, fhall hurry him on board a fhip, and confign him to the care of an American planter for the reft of his days; the cafe of Hagar, will, according to his own explanation of it, be as good an authority for this proceeding, as when it was introduced to give a fanction to the African Slave Trade.

L E T. T E R III.

————————

I F you will keep in view the diſtinction between a blind and ſuperſtitious ad-
miſſion, that every fact authoriſed in the
Old and New Teſtament, is to be taken
as a rule of conduct, without any con-
ſideration of concurrent circumſtances;
and the reaſonable and orthodox conſtruction of the ſcriptures, which I have
contended for, viz. That determinations in particular circumſtances, and
under ſo peculiar a diſpenſation as that
of the Jews, can be no authority for
general conduct; you will hold in your
hand a clue, which will ſafely guide you
through all the windings and intricacies

of

of Mr. H's *labyrinth*, and will find, that every other authority he has quoted, will, when examined by this rule, have as little weight in juftifying the principle of the Slave Trade, as the ftory of Abram and Hagar.

For inftance,—the hiftory of Jofeph's hoarding the corn, and afterwards felling it to the Egyptians, contains a great variety of particular circumftances; all of them intirely different from any thing in the African Slave Trade. Jofeph had forefeen the famine, and had prudently made a referve of corn during the feven years of plenty; by which he had moft probably faved the lives of the greateft part of the inhabitants; but have the merchants of Europe ever conferred a fimilar obligation on the natives of Africa? The purchafe of this corn muft have amounted to a confiderable fum of money,

money, which had been circulated amongſt
the Egyptians; and Joſeph was therefore
in ſome reſpects juſtified in reſelling the
corn, and perhaps at an advanced price.
But have *ſuch* of the natives of Africa as
are reduced to ſlavery, ever received any
kind of compenſation for the deprivation
of every thing dear to them ? In the
event it turns out that Joſeph did not reduce the Egyptians to a ſtate of actual
bondage; but that he entered into a com-
pact with them, viz. That he ſhould
give them feed to ſow the land, and that
they ſhould have *four parts* of the produce, and Pharaoh the fifth part.

Not one of the inhabitants was ſold to
any diſtant country, nor ever removed
out of the kingdom of Egypt; nor does
it appear, that any other end was effected
by this tranſaction, than merely the levy-
ing a tax of one fifth of the produce
throughout

throughout the kingdom.* No fubfequent notice being taken in the facred books, that the inhabitants of Egypt were held in flavery by their own Kings; on the contrary, it appears that in the following reign, the Egyptians had reduced into flavery the children of Ifrael, and acted the part of tafk-mafters over them.†

What then fhall we think of the reafonablenefs and modefty of Mr. H.? who has thought it neceffary to employ his time in making a calculation of the number of inhabitants at that period in Egypt; which he finds to have amounted to feven or eight millions, and which he fuppofes is a number not unequal to all the purchafes of the kind ever made by Englifh merchants, fince the commencement of the flave trade!

After

* Gen. c. xlvii, v. 26.　† Ex. c. i. v. 8.

After all—will it be faid, that under the light we now enjoy in the chriftian difpenfation, the conduct of Jofeph ought to be a rule for the conduct of the governor of a country in modern times; even fuppofing it poffible the fame events fhould again come to pafs? Would it be confiftent with the very pofitive injunction of our Lord, " *Give to him that afketh thee, and from him that would borrow of thee turn not thou away?*"* The withholding the corn till the people furrendered their lands, and even their perfonal liberties, implies *a right* in Jofeph (though at that time the Governor, and confequently the protector of the country) to withhold the corn, *even though the inhabitants fhould perifh for want of it.*— A pofition which may well be doubted. And, granting the ftory in the extent Mr. H. requires, where was the policy or ad-

G   vantage

* Mat. c. v, v. 42.

vantage in Pharaoh being a *Slave-holder* or *Tyrant*, rather than the king of a happy and independent people.

If then the inftance of Jofeph's conduct towards the Egyptians would not in modern times, under the light of the Gofpel, be a fanction for the ruler of a country under fimilar circumftances, to follow his example—how, in the name of common fenfe, can it be an authority for the *Slave Trade?* By which, without any pretence of compenfation, the inhabitants of Africa are carried away from their native country, and compelled to intenfe labour; with no further allowance than what is barely fufficient to fupport their exiftence? The inhabitants of Egypt enjoyed *four-fifths of the produce of the land*; their countrymen in modern times are not allowed *one fiftieth*. Pharaoh we are told was hard of heart.

What

What then shall we think of the present system of Slavery?

From these instances of Hagar and of Joseph, Mr. H. informs us, he thinks he has sufficiently demonstrated that the Slave Trade has the indisputable sanction of Divine Authority, and is in exact conformity with the principles of the law of nature, as delineated in the sacred writings of the word of God. But whether such reasoning would not disgrace any cause, except the cause it is intended to defend, I leave you to judge.

I now come to that part of Mr. H's work, in which he attempts to shew, that the slave trade is in conformity with the principles of the *Mosaic law*. That such was the practice amongst the Israelites, and that such practice was allowed under the Mosaic institution, I have al-

ready

ready admitted: but before I enter further into the difcuffion of this part of the queftion, I fhall beg leave to make one obfervation on the only hiftorical fact cited by Mr. H. under the law as an authority for flavery, viz. that of Jofhua's treatment of the inhabitants of Gibeon.

The facred writings inform us, that the land of Gibeon was given to the children of Ifrael, who were authorized *by an exprefs revelation from God*, to deftroy all the inhabitants of the land.* For what particular crimes in the nations adjacent to the Ifraelites thefe heavy judgements were denounced againft them, does not appear; fuch however was the power and authority with which Jofhua was invefted at the time the event cited by Mr. H. took place.

But

* Jofh. c. i. v. 2. 3. and c. ix. v. 24.

But where is the revelation by which the inhabitants of Africa are delivered up to the people of Europe? Where is the authority of the kingdom of England over that of Angola? Whence is it derived? Who hath ever heard it afferted? Or in what writings, facred or prophane, is it to be found?

This circumftance, then, which is the *foundation* and *fole juftification* of Jofhua's fubfequent conduct, being wanting in the cafe to which it is now applied, intirely deftroys all fimilarity between them.

For the Gibeonites having been abfolutely delivered up to the power of Jofhua, who was authorifed, and even commanded to deftroy them; he could, with the permiffion of God, change that feverity of treatment to a milder punifhment; and from fuch change, the Gibeonites derived

a great,

a great advantage, viz. the prefervation of their lives. But have the Slave dealers of Europe faved from deftruction and extirpation any of the nations of Africa? Have the judgments of God been denounced againft thofe people, and have fuch judgments been averted by the humanity or interference of the Europeans? On the contrary, have they not, for ages paft, in oppofition to the pofitive laws of God, in open contempt of the Chriftian religion, and without any other authority than that of being the ftrongeft, defolated and difpeopled one of the moft populous and fertile parts of the univerfe? Whether this has given them a right, equal to that of Jofhua over the Gibeonites, I leave to Mr. H. to explain. I muft however agree with him in thinking, *that it is eafy to conclude, whether the reducing the innocent as well as the guilty part of our fellow creatures to the*

condition

condition of flaves, or even to hereditary bondage or flavery, be in its own nature licit, or illicit, criminal, or unjuft. And I truft that no perfon who has candidly attended to the fubject in difpute can have a doubt upon the queftion.

L E T-

I HAVE already admitted, that the practice of flavery was permitted to the Ifraelites and their immediate anceftors:— But I have at the fame time afferted, that fuch permiffion *was confined to that people only*, and was not extended to the reft of mankind. I fhall now undertake to fhew, that the practice of flavery, as allowed to the Ifraelites, fo far from receiving a fanction from, was abolifhed by the Chriftian difpenfation, as being totally irreconcileable with the firft principles of the religion of its divine author.

Mr.

Mr. H. has endeavoured to intrench himſelf, by every precaution in his power, againſt the attack, which he well knew his cauſe was expoſed to receive from. this quarter, and has ſtipulated, that the books of the Old and New Teſtament, ſhall be conſidered as of equal authority. But if Mr. H. be as fully ſatisfied as he pretends to be, that the doctrines of our Saviour are uniformly of the ſame tendency as thoſe of the Moſaic Law, why does he ſo earneſtly labour to eſtabliſh a propoſition, which the greateſt part of his readers will ſcarcely be inclined to grant him? Does he not appear to have been aware, not only that his cauſe would derive no authority from the New Teſtament, but that the diſpenſations of the new law, might in ſome reſpects interfere with and contradict thoſe of the Old?

H   That

That this may reasonably be presumed to be Mr. H's true motive for endeavouring to establish the equal authority of the Old and New Testament, will appear from considering the reason he gives, for having been more particular in bringing the last part of his researches into what he calls a central point of view, viz. " That he has reason to apprehend, that " several of his readers would be apt to " imagine, that by the establishment of " the Christian Religion the Law of " Moses was totally abolished, and an- " nulled in every part of it; and to every " intent and purpose, both typical and " moral." Now it is impossible for Mr. " H. to be so ignorant as not to know, that every sect and denomination of Christians admit the moral precepts of the Old Testament, whenever they do not interfere with the purer doctrines of the Christian scheme—this then could not be

the

the true motive for his being fo particular on this head. The fact is, he hoped that by eftablifhing the equality of the Old Teftament to the New, he could with more advantage make the authorities which he pretended to find in the former, for the general juftification of flavery, mili- tate againft the exprefs and unequivocal precepts againft it, which are contained in the latter.

Of what great importance the eftablifh- ment of this propofition is to Mr. H's argument, will appear from the ufe he has attempted to make of it. " From " this undeniable pofition, fays he, it " follows neceffarily, that *as the writ-* " *ings of both the Teftaments have the* " *fame weight of authority*, effentially in- " capable of contradicting itfelf, in fup- " port of thofe principles and decifions " enacted and regiftered in their refpective " records, concerning the intrinfic mo-

" rality

" rality or immorality of human actions,
" whatever is declared in the one to be
" intrinsically good or bad, just or un-
" just, licit or illicit, must inevitably
" be so *according to the principles of the*
" *other*. If therefore the Slave Trade
" appears, *as I trust it does*, from the
" preceding train of Scriptural Argu-
" ments, in perfect harmony with the
" principles and decisions of the word
" of God, registered in the sacred writ-
" ings of the Old Testament, respect-
" ing the intrinsic nature of that trade,
" this of course can bear no opposition
" to, but must necessarily be in equal
" perfect harmony with the principles
" and decisions of the word of God, re-
" specting right and justice,—registered
" in the sacred writings of the New.
" This general but forcible argument,
" were it even unsupported by any col-
" lateral evidences from the writings of
" the New Testament, would be fully

" sufficient

" sufficient to verify my third and last
" assertion respecting the licitness of the
" Slave Trade, as perfectly conformable
" to the principles of the Christian dif-
" pensation.

Thus Mr. H. has reposed the whole
weight of his argument in favour of the
Slave Trade, under the Christian dif-
pensation (as unsupported by any collateral evidence from the writings of the
New Testament) on this single proposi-
tion, " *that the writings of both the Tes-
taments have the same weight of authority.*" I shall therefore first proceed to
give the most indubitable evidence that
this is not the fact; and that the New
Testament *not only possesses, but has exercised* a controlling power over the Old,
even in points of moral conduct, in conse-
quence of which, " This general and
" forcible argument, which is itself suf-
" ficient

" ficient to verify the affertion that the
" licitnefs of the Slave Trade is perfectly
" conformable to the principles of the
" Chriftian difpenfation," will be found
" entirely groundlefs ; — after which I
fhail proceed to confider what he calls his
collateral evidences derived from the New
Teftament. _

After having, with fome indecency of
expreffion, afferted that " God never did,
nor ever could, alter by any difpenfation whatever, thofe eternal principles
and laws, which are the very bafis and
foundation of true religion ; and confe-
fequently of the religion of Chrift," he
adduces, as he fays, " no lefs an autho-
" rity in confirmation of this indifputable
" doctrine, than the very words of the
" Son of God, who in that divine fer-
" mon on the mount, in which he gave
" his difciples a moft minute and circum-
ftantial

" ftantial account of the principles and
" tenets of his gofpel, condemned the
" above erroneous opinion in the moft
" explicit terms, and forbad them even
" to think of it. *Think not, faid he, that*
" *I am come to deftroy the law or the*
" *prophets; I came not to deftroy but to*
" *fulfil.*"

This being the only authority produced by Mr. H. in fupport of his affertion, of *the equality of the Old and
New Teftament*, I fhall firft point out,
what I conceive to be the true purport of that paffage; and fhall afterwards produce fuch authorities, in fupport of my opinion, as I think the
warmeft friends of Mr. H. muft admit to
be decifive on the point in queftion.

" *Think not, fays our Saviour, that I*
" *am come to deftroy the law and the pro-*
" *phets;*

" *phets; I am not come to deftroy but to*
" *fulfil.*"

By which is clearly to be underftood,
that he came not to overthrow thofe firft
principles of morality, which are inculcated in the Old Teftament, *but to im-
prove and carry them to a higher degree
of perfection*; and accordingly in the fe-
of his difcourfe, he adverts to *many
actions and modes of conduct* which were
permitted under the old law, but which
he declares are *improper*, and *actually prohibits, thereby making a moft effential difference between the morality of the* Old
Teftament and that of the new.

Matt. c. v. v. 21. " Ye have heard that
" it was faid by them of old time, thou
" fhalt not kill; and whofoever fhall kill,
" fhall be in danger of the judgment.

22. But

" 22. But I fay unto you, that who-
" foever is angry with his brother with-
" out a caufe, fhall be in danger of the
" judgment, &c.

" 27. Ye have heard that it was faid
" by them of old time, thou fhalt not
" commit adultery.

" 28. But I fay unto you, that who-
" foever looketh on a woman to luft after
" her, hath committed adultery already
" with her in his heart.

" 38. Ye have heard that it hath
" been faid, an eye for an eye, and a
" tooth for a tooth.—

" 39. But I fay unto you, that ye
" refift not evil; but whofoever fhall
" fmite thee on thy right cheek, turn to
" him the other alfo.

I   " 43. Ye

" 43. Ye have heard that it have
" been faid, thou fhalt love thy neigh-
" bour and hate thine enemy.

" 44. But I fay unto you, *love your*
" *enemies, blefs them that curfe you, and*
" *pray for them which defpitefully ufe*
" *you and perfecute you.*"

Could any doubt remain after confidering the foregoing paffage, as to the meaning of our Saviour's declaration, that *he
came not to deftroy but to fulfil,* or the
fuperior and controlling power of the
Chriftian difpenfation, the following explicit declaration of the apoftle Paul,
upon the fubject, will perhaps have as
much weight as the pofitive affertions of
Mr. H. to the contrary.

Heb. c. 7. v. 18. " *For there is verily*
" *a difannulling of the commandment going*
" *before*

" *before, for the weaknefs and unprofita-*
" *blenefs thereof.*

" 19. For *the law made nothing per-*
" *fect,* but the bringing in of a better
" hope *did,* by the which we draw nigh
" unto God.

" 22. By fo much was Jefus made a
" furety of *a better Teftament.*"

Thus then it appears to demonftration,
that the Chriftian religion, is not only
fuperior to the Mofaic inftitution, but
that it's authority was exerted to change
or make void, or in the words of the
apoftle, " *to difannul the command-*
ment going before;" and confequently all
denominations of Chriftians muft admit,
that wherever the fanctions and ordinances of the Old Teftament, interfere
with the purer doctrines and more hu-

mane

mane precepts of the New, they are not to be regarded as of fufficient weight to juſtify the followers of Chriſt, in the imitation of them.

Nor is it from this circumſtance to be preſumptuouſly inferred (as Mr. H. affects to think) " That God is not confiſtent " with himſelf; or that the religion of " the New Teſtament, inſtead of being " the perfection and accompliſhment, is " the reproach and condemnation of the " old law." The Moſaic inſtitution was not of general import, but was principally confined to the Jews; and contained regulations, both of a civil and religious nature, proper to that people, under a Theocratic Government, but inapplicable in many inſtances to mankind in general.—Nor was it in many reſpects ſo pure and perfect in its moral precepts, as that with which mankind were afterwards favoured.

favoured. Upon this point the teſtimony of the apoſtle Paul, in his Epiſtle to the Galatians (who appear to have receded from the goſpel diſpenſation to the inadequate precepts of the old law) is ſo peculiarly applicable, that I cannot avoid citing it as a full anſwer to Mr. Harris's charge of inconſiſtency in the Old and New Teſtaments.

Galatians c. 3. v. 19. " *Wherefore then* " *ſerveth the law?* It was added becauſe " of tranſgreſſions, till the ſeed ſhould " come to whom the promiſe was made, " and it was ordained by angels in the " hand of a mediator.

" 21. *Is the law then againſt the pro-* " *miſes of God?* God forbid—for if there " had been a law given, *which could* " *have given life*—verily *righteouſneſs* " *ſhould have been by the law.*

" 22. But

" 22. But the fcripture hath concluded
" all under fin—that the promife by faith
" of Jefus Chrift might be given to them
" that believe.

" 23. But *before faith came* we were
" kept under the law, fhut up unto the
" faith, which fhould afterwards be re-
" vealed.

" 24. Wherefore *the law was our fchool*
" *mafter* to bring us unto Chrift, that
" we might be juftified by faith.

" 25. But *after that faith is come we*
" *are no longer under a fchoolmafter.*"

From this paffage then it will appear,
that the daring accufation thrown out
by Mr. H. that the Supreme Being
is inconfiftent with himfelf, becaufe
he

he did not, under the Chriftian difpenfation, confirm and confine himfelf
to every moral injunction of the Old
Teftament, can only be made *fuch perfons*,
as having for interefted purpofes attempted
to eftablifh a fyftem which the evident
purport of the Scriptures cannot fupport;
have no method to hide their difgrace, but
by this direct and dreadful imputation on
the facred writings and their Divine author.

It is alfo eqaully evident from the
foregoing paffages of the New Teftament,
not only that the moral prohibitions of
our Saviour extended further than the in-
junctions of the old law, and rendered
that conduct *unlawful*, which had before
been permitted, but that fuch prohibitions actually extended to the particular
cafe in queftion, and that *all practices*,
inimical to the general welfare and in-
terefts

terefts of mankind, were from thence-
forth to be abolifhed; for *if it be the duty
of a Chriftian not to refift evil—to love his
enemies — to blefs thofe that curfe, and
pray for thofe who perfecute him,—how
can it be fuppofed that he fhall at the fame
time have an inherent right to do evil to
another—to injure thofe who never injured
him—and to deftroy thofe, who fo far from
having either perfecuted, or curfed him,
have never known that fuch a perfon was
in exiftence ?*

I do not conceive it neceffary to follow
Mr. H. through the *tedious argument*, by
which he labours to prove, that the filence of the New Teftament refpecting
the Slave Trade, (fuppofing it to be filent
on the fubject) is a virtual approbation
of that practice. The New Teftament
is totally filent on many *crimes* of the
greateft magnitude, if fuch filence is to be
inferred

inferred from its not containing *particular prohibitions againft them*;—but will any perfon contend that fuch crimes are lawful, becaufe no fpecific denunciations are pronounced againft them by our Saviour? Or are they not underftood to be included in thofe general prohibitions and commands, to love our neighbour as ourfelves, which compofe the fum and effence of the Chriftian religion?

But if the Books of the New Teftament be filent on many particular offences, they lay down general and moft powerful precepts for the regulation of the heart and life, leaving the profeffors of Chriftianity to apply thefe precepts to particular cafes; and they who have imbibed the true fpirit of charity, breathed in the gofpel, will not find it neceffary to adopt a long train of reafoning, in order to perceive whether the *Slave Trade* be lawful, or not; but as foon as they underftand its nature and

K   confe-

confequences, will feel a lively conviction, *that chriftianity abhors the practice.*

The implied arguments of Mr. H. in favour of the Slave Trade, from *the exact conformity of the moral precepts of the New Teftament with thofe of the Old,* and from *the filence of the New Teftament on that fpecific crime,* being thus fufficiently refuted; it may now be proper to turn to what he calls his collateral proofs from the New Teftament, or thofe paffages which he pretends afford a pofitive fanction to the Slave Trade, under the New Law.

This fanction he conceives he has found in two of the Epiftles of Paul, viz. The 1ft of thofe to Tim. c. vi. v. 1, and that to Philemon, v. 8.

But what fhall we fay, if this flender twig,

twig, which is now the only support of the sinking advocate of Slavery, should desert him; and it should appear, from a candid and dispassionate examination of the passages in question, that the precepts of the apostle, introduced by Mr. H. to justify a course of conduct in direct opposition to the precepts of Christianity, afford not the slightest inference inimical to the general rules of good will and benevolence inculcated in other parts of the New Testament.

In the passage first cited by Mr. H. Tim. c. vi. v. 1, the apostle Paul exhorts " as many as are under the yoke, to count " their masters worthy of all honour, that " the name of God and his doctrine be " not blasphemed; and that they who " have believing masters, should not des- " pise them, because they are brethren, " but rather do them service, &c." —

K 2

From

From whence he infers, " that the pri-
" mitive Chriftians were not only not
" forbidden, but *exprefsly allowed*, by
" the principles of our religion, the pur-
" chafing of flaves, and keeping their
" fellow creatures, nay, even their fel-
" low chriftians, under the yoke of bon-
" dage or flavery."

Now taking for granted, what perhaps
may well be difputed, that the perfons
fpoken of in this paffage were flaves for
life,—it muft be remembered, that the
great author of the Chriftian fyftem did
not think proper to oppofe his authority
to the political arrangements which at the
time of his miffion fubfifted on the face
of the earth. His doctrines always inculcated fubmiffion to fuperiors, and pa-
tience under injuries ; and this doctrine
the apoftle applies in the prefent inftance,
to a particular clafs of perfons, to whom
he

he thought fuch admonitions were neceffary; requiring them " to count their
mafters worthy of all honour," meaning
thereby, that during the continuance of
their fervitude (the origin, nature, or
duration of which does not appear,) they
fhould perform their duty, and patiently
fubmit to the fituation in which they were
placed; but by no means juftifying any
perfon *who held another in illegal or forcible fubjection*. The apoftle exhorts thefe
fervants to account their mafters worthy
of all honour, that the name of God
and his doctrine be not blafphemed; *but*
which Chriftian like fubmiffion, and for-
bearance, *though an act of virtue in the
fervant*, could by no means *juftify*, but
would rather tend to aggravate, the crime
of the mafter. In exact conformity to
this doctrine is the precept of our Saviour, " *If any one ftrike thee on thy right
cheek, turn to him the other alfo.*" But
will

will Mr. H. maintain that it is lawful to
ftrike a Chriftian, becaufe his religion
commands him not to refift evil ? Or is
it not rather the higheft aggravation, that
the meek and peaceable deportment of the
perfon offended, could not fecure him
from infult and abufe ?

The long quotation Mr. H. has made
from the Epiftle of Paul to Philemon, is
fo far from being a juftification of flavery,
that to every perfon not perufing the fcriptures with a particular bias on his mind, it
is evidently a powerful exhortation againft
it. The apoftle fends back Onefimus to
his mafter, requefting him to receive him,
" *not as a fervant, but above a fervant* ;
" a *brother beloved*, efpecially to me, but
" how much more unto thee, *both in the*
" *flefh and in the Lord.*" Where does the
apoftle addrefs Philemon in the words ex-
preffly attributed to him by Mr. H. " *that*
he

he would never attempt to deprive him of his slave?" Where does he acknowledge to Philemon, " that Onefimus is his own brother in Chrift, though *ftill his property according to the flefh?"* . Thefe paffages feem to be the laft refort of a perfon, who, not being able to fupport his affertion from the evident purport of the words, is obliged to have recourfe to *forgery and interpolation.*

Such however are the grounds upon which Mr. H. has ventured to infringe upon the pofitive commands of our Saviour, with refpect to our conduct towards each other;—but an apprehenfion arifing in his mind, that thefe paffages might, after all the pains employed in inforcing them, be infufficient to anfwer his purpofe, whilft the precepts of good will given to mankind in the New Teftament remained unimpeached—he finds

it

it neceffary, in the laft place, to abridge the purport of thefe precepts, and to weaken their influence. For this purpofe, he felects out of the many fimilar paffages which the New Teftament affords, one which he conceives may bear a more li- mitted fenfe ; and be explained in fuch a manner, as not to appear inconfiftent with his favourite eftablifhment. Whether he has been fortunate in his felection will appear from a fhort inveftigation.

Matt. c. vii. v. 12. " All things " whatfoever ye would that men fhould " do to you, do ye even fo to them ; for " this is the law and the prophets."

This divine precept, delivered by Chrift to his difciples at the conclufion of his fermon on the mount, is fo ftrict an in- junction againft every kind of injuftice and oppreffion ; expreffed in a manner fo

forcible,

forcibly, and preſcribing a teſt of our conduct ſo eaſily applied upon every occaſion, that Mr. H. was aware it could not be overlooked in this controverſy; and he has accordingly employed the utmoſt of his ſophiſtry to evade its import.

After ſtating the paſſage, he gives the converſe of it in the following words.

" Whatſoever things therefore we
" would not that men ſhould do to us,
" we are not even ſo to do to them; but
" no perſon whatever would certainly
" wiſh that a fellow creature ſhould re-
" duce him to the condition of a ſlave,
" therefore no perſon whatever is to re-
" duce a fellow creature to that con-
" dition."

" Here, ſays he, I muſt obſerve, that

L   " no.

" no one can juftly tax me with any
" partiality to the caufe I have efpoufed;
" I have, I think, worded the argument
" againft it, in terms as forcible as the
" moft zealous advocate for African li-
" berty could ufe; but unanfwerable as
" the fame may appear to them, it is but
" *a plaufible argument at the beft.*

" It is an axiom in logic, that an ar-
" gument that proves too much, proves
" nothing—*the above is juft fuch a one;*
" for by the fame manner of reafoning,
" one might equally conclude, contrary
" to the law, and the prophets, and the
" doctrine of the Chriftian Religion, that
" not only flavery, but every other kind
" of fubordination of one man to ano-
" ther, ought not to be fuffered to con-
" tinue in the world. The argument, if
" conclufive in the former cafe, muft be
" equally

" equally fo in the latter. I enforce it
" thus:—

" *All things whatfoever*, fays our
" bleffed Saviour, *that men fhould do to*
" *you, do ye even fo to them, for this is*
" *the law and the prophets.* Whatfoever
" things therefore we would not that
" men fhould do to us, we are not even
" fo to do to them; but every perfon
" would naturally wifh not to be con-
" trouled by a fellow creature, not to
" be *under any fubjection* to him, but to
" be abfolute mafter of his own actions;
" no perfon therefore ought to keep a fel-
" low creature under any controul or fub-
" jection whatever."

Surely fo manifeft a perverfion of the
precepts of Chrift, never before difgraced
the prefs. *It is not true* that every perfon would wifh *not to be controuled by a*

fellow

fellow creature, nor to be under any sub-jection to him, but to be absolute master of his own actions. Every man of common sense knows, that from the constitution of the universe, he is dependant on, and must necessarily in many respects be con-trouled by others ; and none but an ideot would wish to be discharged from the re-lative duties of life, and to be absolute master of his own actions. Nor is any situation in life exempt from this general law, which by an interchange of good offices binds together the vast fabrick of society—but every man may reasonably object to his being *forcibly reduced to a state of slavery,* and deprived of those natural rights which the rest of mankind enjoy—a state which so far from occasion-ing an interchange of good offices, gives rise on the one hand only to pride, cruelty and injustice ; and on the other, to fear, meanness, and hatred. It does not then

by

by any means follow, that *becaufe* mankind have an uniform averfion to a ftate
of flavery, they have *therefore* a diflike
to all the other natural and juft fubor-
dinations and dependencies of life; and
Mr. H's impeachment of this precept
is therefore as unfounded as all his other
attempts to explain away the evident purport of the doctrines of the New Teftament.

Having found that the fenfe evidently
implied in, and univerfally underftood
from thefe words, is not the true one,
he gives us his own definition of it.———
" Every Chriftian, fays he, is taught and
" directed to do unto others as he would
" be done unto, and by a neceffary
" confequence, not to do unto others as
" he would not be done unto;—that is,
" fays he, every Chriftian is commanded
" to behave to his neighbour in what-
" ever

" ever situation or circumstances in life
" *providence may have placed them both,*
" just as he would wish his neighbour to
" behave to him, in his situation, were
" his neighbour's situation and circum-
" stances his own." Despicable evasion!
Wretched sophistry! Shall a man, who
has voluntarily and forcibly reduced another to a state of the most abject misery
of which his nature is capable, impiously
affert that *providence has placed him in
that situation?* Shall he satisfy himself
with the plausible pretext of acting with
kindness towards him, whilst he has it in
his power to extend to him that mercy
which *in the same situation he would himself most ardently wish for.* As well might
the midnight murderer, who holds the
knife over the innocent victim of his cruelty, assert that *providence had delivered
him into his hands,* and claim a merit in
putting him to death with as little pain

as

as poffible. Surely if it be the duty of a Chriftian, to relieve thofe who are in fituations of diftrefs, it is *not lefs* in-cumbent on him to place them in a bet-ter fituation, as often as it lies in his power.

That the Chriftian religion is inimical in its nature to every fpecies of oppref-fion, and particularly to that which in-volves in it almoft every other kind of guilt, is I hope already evident. But as a further confirmation of this fentiment, it may not be improper to fhew, what has been the general fenfe of mankind as to the fpirit and purport of the Chriftian religion. So oppofite are its precepts to the encouragement of flavery, that a ce-lebrated hiftorian,* has not fcrupled to account for the degree of liberty, which is at prefent enjoyed throughout moft

parts

* Robertfon's Hift. Charles V. Proofs and illuft. v. 1, note 20.

parts of Europe, from the influence of this religion on the minds of the people. —I fhall give you the paffage.—

" The gentle fpirit of the Chriftian
" religion, together with the doctrines
" which it teaches concerning the ori-
" ginal equality of mankind, as well
" as the impartial eye with which the
" Almighty regards men of every con-
" dition, and admits them to a partici-
" pation of his benefits, are inconfiftent
" with fervitude; but in this, as in many
" other inftances, *confiderations of intereft,*
" and *the maxims of falfe policy,* led men
" to a conduct inconfiftent with their
" principles. They were fo fenfible,
" however, of their inconfiftency, that
" to fet their fellow Chriftians at liberty
" from fervitude, was deemed an act of
" piety highly meritorious and accept-
" able to heaven. The *humane fpirit*
" *of the Chriftian religion* ftruggled with
the

" the maxims and manners of the world,
" and *contributed more than any other*
" *circumſtance to introduce the practice*
" *of manumiſſion.*"

The ſame author furniſhes us with an authentic document, as a proof of this fact; which as it proceeds from the apoſtolic chair, will have its due weight with Mr. H. It contains the reaſons aſſigned by Pope Gregory the Great, in the ſixth century, for granting liberty to his ſlaves.

" Cum Redemptor noſter, totius con-
" ditor naturæ, ad hoc propitiatus, hu-
" manam carnem voluerit aſſumere, ut
" divinitatis ſuæ gratia, dirempto (quo
" tenebamur captivi) vinculo, priſtinæ
" nos reſtituerit libertati; ſalubriter agiter,
" ſi homines, *quos ab initio liberos na-*
" *tura protulit,* & jus gentium jugo ſub-

M   " ſtituit

" ftituit fervitutis, in ea qua nati fue-
" rant, manumittentis beneficio, libertate
" reddantur."*

And the ufual tenor of the charters
of manumiffion is—*pro amore dei*—*pro re-*
medio animæ, &c. clearly expreffing the
fenfe the inhabitants of Europe have entertained, that the manumiffion of flaves
was an act *in conformity to the precepts*
of the Chriftian religion.

Were I to continue thefe authorities
down to the prefent times, and cite to
Mr. H. the opinions of the many re-
fpectable clergymen of every fect in thefe
kingdoms

* Seeing that Jefus Chrift, the author of all nature, for
this exprefs purpofe, affumed the flefh, that by the favour
of his divine power (the bonds of captivity being broken)
he might reftore us to our former liberty : We conceive it
to be devoutly done, if, by the favour of manumiffion,
MEN, whom nature originally made free, and human laws
fubjected to the yoke of fervitude, were again reftored to
that liberty in which they were born.

kingdoms who have oppofed this unlawful traffic; fome of them *folely and expreſſly* on the ground of its being contrary to the dictates of the Chriſtian Religion, they would perhaps have little weight with him; but with the rational and difpaſſionate part of mankind, they will not be without their effect; and will be no inconfiderable authority, towards the deduction which I conceive I may fairly be allowed to make from the foregoing remarks, viz. THAT THE PRACTICE OF SLAVERY, AS ALLOWED AMONGST THE JEWS, WAS ABROGATED BY THE GOSPEL DISPENSATION, AND DOES NOT NOW EXIST EITHER IN THEIR IMMEDIATE DESCENDANTS OR IN ANY OTHER PEOPLE.

If Mr. H. remains diſſatisfied with a conclufion in fuch direct oppofition to the *long corollaries* at the end of his book,

he

he muſt contend, that the particular privilege granted to the Jews, and their an-
ceſtors, *is not annulled*, but yet exiſts in
full force. And, as I have before re-
marked, muſt, *if ſuch a privilege be he-*
reditary, inſtitute an enquiry into their
lineal deſcendants, amongſt whom I apprehend he will find ſome difficulty in
inrolling the inhabitants of theſe kingdoms.

But if he denies alſo this laſt propoſition ; and aſſerts that the permiſſion of
holding others in ſlavery, was given in-
diſcriminately to all mankind ; I muſt
beg you once more to conſider for a moment *the conſequences and abſurdities of*
ſuch a poſition. If all mankind *poſſeſs from*
God, an *inherent right to reduce into ſub-*
jection any others of their ſpecies, this
right is inherent *as well in the ſlave as in*
his maſter, who will therefore be perfectly
juſtified

juftified in making ufe of his utmoft ex-
ertions to *change fituations with him*; and
fhould he fucceed in his attempt, will,
in his turn, have " the pofitive fanction
of God," for *holding by force his former
mafter in fubjection to him*. Thus then
this univerfal permiffion or *licitnefs* of
flavery, contended for by the author of
the pamphlet, terminates in a vindication
of univerfal oppreffion,—in an affertion
of the right of the ftronger, at all times
to injure and opprefs the weaker. In
fhort, in a general annihilation of all
thofe reftraints, which Law, Reafon,
Religion, and Common Senfe, have hi-
therto impofed upon mankind.

T H E   E N D.

www.ingramcontent.com/pod-product-compliance
Lightning Source LLC
Chambersburg PA
CBHW021421090426
42742CB00009B/1210